My Servants

Would Be

Fighting

A Meditation on the Gospel
and the Kingdoms of the World

Storm Bailey

VIDE

Vide Press
6200 Second Street
Washington D.C. 20011
www.VidePress.com

ISBN: 978-1-954618-16-9 (Print)
ISBN: 978-1-954618-17-6 (ebook)

Printed in the United States of America

Cover by Miblart.com
Cover image used is in the Public Domain

Table of Contents

Preface

I know that most of us—left, right, and center—are deeply invested in our approach to politics: in the positions we have taken, and in the causes that strike us as most essential. Let's take a step back from all that. I'm not going to try and tell you who to vote for, or who you should've voted for, or what political parties you should be for or against. But I do want to offer you *something* … otherwise, why should you bother to read this book? What will that be? A vision. A meditation on the scriptures, with particular attention to what the Bible seems to say about the church, the kingdom of God, and the gospel. My hope is that a fresh look at the implications of that will, under the guidance of the Spirit of God, inform and infuse our deepest attitudes toward politics and the nations of the world. The goal is not that we get politics right, but that—whatever we do in politics—we portray the gospel with power and accuracy, in our individual testimonies and lives and in our collective life as the body of Christ on earth.

There is an implicit judgment in all of this: I don't think that we are accurately representing the gospel all the time. If there is a tendency or theme in that misrepresentation, it's that we make it look as if the gospel and the kingdom of God are only about *this* world. On trial before Pilate, Jesus told him, "My kingdom is not of this world. If My kingdom were of this world, then My servants would be fighting so that I would not be handed over to the Jews; but as it is, My kingdom is not of this realm."

I'll tell you plainly that I think sometimes it looks today as if the servants of Jesus are fighting—just as if his kingdom was "of this realm." If this is true, it is true of Christians all along the political spectrum—not just the left and not just the right. So, again, I'm not taking sides on that. And I'm also not claiming that the gospel and the kingdom of God have no application in this world—in fact, the opposite is true. If we truly serve Christ, then love for our neighbor may well demand more of us in hard daily service to the world than many of us—including me—are doing now. I want to be open to that as we study the scripture, and I want to be sensitive to the way that self-interest (loving my own life, comfort, and reputation) can distort my thinking and shape my interpretation of what it means to be a disciple of Jesus in this time and this place. For the sake of the gospel, my prayer is that the Holy Spirit enlighten and guide me as the writer and you as the reader.

A little bit of truth in advertising:

The cords of death encompassed me
And the terrors of the nether world came upon me;
I found distress and sorrow.
Then I called upon the name of the Lord:
"O Lord, I beseech You, save my life!" (Psalm 116)

When I became a Christian, I was eighteen years old, on the road, with not much to lose. It was 1975, and I had grown up watching the "counterculture" loudly reject the inherited patterns of American life. I thought they were right about the emptiness of consumer culture, about the lack of reasons offered for moral rules, and about the poverty of cultural conformity. I still think so. I also thought they were right that drugs, lawlessness, and thoughtless anti-authoritarianism were the key features of a new and better social order. I could not have been more wrong. I went from an idealistic ten-year-old watching news clips of the summer of love to a broken eighteen-year-old, kicked out of school, meaningful relationships eroded, and a slave to drugs that were destroying my mind and body ... and that I spent every waking minute using or seeking.

Like I said, I had nothing to lose.

The Lord preserves the simple;
I was brought low, and He saved me.

When the gospel of Jesus Christ came to me—suddenly, unlooked for—I was transformed by an encounter with the living truth. Awakened to the horror of my moral depravity, I cried out to God to be saved and, against all hope or reason, I was. Guided by providence, I found my way across the country and into a group of souls like me—mostly drug people, young outsiders, trying to learn to live survivable lives as followers of Jesus.

Here's where the truth in advertising comes in. It was, in one sense, easy for us to take the radical message of Jesus in the New Testament at face value. Leave everything and follow Me? Hey, we already left everything … for nothing. The Son of Man has no place to lay his head? I slept on the ground hitchhiking to get here. For us, the church became a community of outcasts, committed to each other and to Jesus all the time, every day. This isn't to say we didn't have stuff to forsake—sex, drugs, and lawlessness—and not all of us managed to keep our hands to the plow. But, for the aforementioned really stupid reasons, my life as a Christian has never really been caught up in social and cultural expectations about what Christianity is supposed to be. That makes it relatively easy for me to embrace and proclaim the "radical" nature of New Testament discipleship (easy in the cultural sense, I hasten to say, not in the moral sense of a heart devoted to God).

And look, even culturally, I got with the program: my wife and I made homes and raised a family; I went to college (eventually), became a values voter, got a PhD at age forty and wound up a college professor with a couple of cars, a brick house and a retirement account. But I still have, I hope, nothing in this world to lose, and a trace scent of the outsider—out in the weeds where everything depends on Jesus and the world to come, and not so much on the whims and ways of the kingdoms where we find ourselves wandering for a time in exile. This book is a small piece of nearly forty years of teaching in the church. It isn't an academic book and it isn't for academics—except insofar as academics are people like that eighteen-year-old kid: on the road, looking for life, once lost but now found. It is a book about the gospel of Jesus Christ, which is radically different from the world that needs it so desperately.

I.

My Servants Would Be Fighting

Jesus answered, "My kingdom is not of this world. If My kingdom were of this world, then My servants would be fighting so that I would not be handed over to the Jews; but as it is, My kingdom is not of this realm."

John 18:36.

When Jesus was on trial for his life before the Roman governor Pilate, he said that the behavior of his followers was evidence for the kind of kingdom he ruled. If the servants of Jesus *had* been fighting to save Jesus by force, that wouldn't have changed the nature of the kingdom of God, but it would have eliminated that bit of evidence. It might have gone so far as to misrepresent the true nature of the Kingdom.

One thing is for sure: the servants of Jesus are fighting today. That isn't necessarily a bad thing; the New Testament epistles often use the images and language of struggle, right down to swords, armor, and breastplates. But those images aren't about fighting in the way Jesus was talking about, or the way Pilate might have expected; the epistles affirm that "the weapons of our warfare are not carnal, but mighty in the Holy Spirit."

Here is the burden of this book: *the way the servants of Jesus fight is evidence for the kind of kingdom we profess to serve.* What does this mean for our participation in the politics of the earthly kingdoms in which we live? Is it possible that our political actions and attitudes, or what we say about their connection to our Christian faith, could obscure the true nature of God's kingdom, or misrepresent the gospel of Jesus Christ? Even if unintended, that would be tragic beyond words because our neighbors and our world need the gospel and the Kingdom more desperately than they know.

As I write this, such a tragedy is a real and current threat to our testimony. The danger doesn't lie on just one side of the political spectrum—left or right, liberal or conservative. A left-leaning Christian who portrays the biblical concern for the poor as the sole identifying feature of Christianity or Christian political engagement has a concern which is biblical. But it might be expressed with an attitude or approach which obscures the fact that "the kingdom of God is not eating and drinking." What about a conservative Christian who attempts to put the biblical understanding of false gods or sexual purity into law? We know that forcing people outwardly to follow biblical truths will not save them, and might in fact create people like the Pharisees who "clean the outside of the cup, but inside they are full of robbery and self-indulgence." How can Christians live and proclaim the truths of scripture faithfully in the public and political sphere without obscuring the Kingdom or misrepresenting the gospel?

These questions are especially urgent for Christians who have some share in governing—whether by holding office or by having political authority as citizens (like Christians in the United States). This meditation has its roots in the American church—I write out of my own experience. But nothing here depends upon my country, or yours. My aim is to articulate a biblical vision of Christians in the kingdoms of the world, and so the basic principles should be applicable in all times and places; Christians are a people "from every nation, tongue, and tribe."

Trying to spell out principles that can guide us will raise questions and problems that I'll answer as best as I can in the pages that follow. You will be the judge of whether the principles, and solutions to problems, are sound. The standard of judgment for this, obviously, should not be my politics, or yours, but the Bible. That's simple, but also not so simple. In scripture we have a coherent revelation of truth about God and the world by the inspiration of the Holy Spirit, and I affirm this wholeheartedly. But I also admit that my own understanding of what scripture *means* may be flawed. Those flaws are my weakness, not the Bible's. It serves no purpose if anything that I say here is unscriptural; there is plenty of talk about politics which proceeds by setting aside biblical principles, but this book is for Bible-believing Christians.

The aim of this meditation is not to criticize political parties, nor to advocate for or against particular political policies, but to identify guiding biblical principles. We seek a vision of the kingdom of God, and of a commitment to the gospel of Jesus Christ, that takes priority over whatever nation we find ourselves living in, and whatever policies we find ourselves bound by conscience and reflection to support.

In the chapters that follow, we'll look at factors and biblical principles that might shape our attitudes about political participation. Here's an overview of the main ideas:

a) A biblical understanding of humanity means that earthly politics is *tragic*; in most cases this means that any policy decision requires sacrificing some genuine good. That doesn't mean that we can refuse to make policy decisions, but it might mean that God isn't entirely on one side or the other of a policy question.

b) Earthly governments are authorized by God to carry out their responsibilities by force; they "bear the sword," and faithful Christians can share this work. But the kingdom of God, and true religion, is not based on things that can be coerced or legally enforced. The kingdom of God isn't built with the sword. Throughout the history of the church, attempts to build the kingdom that way have obscured—or misrepresented—the gospel of Jesus Christ.

c) Since the kingdom of God is not of this world, no earthly kingdom is God's. The people of God, and the blessing of God, is not nationally defined—even though under the covenant of Moses things were, for purposes of the gospel, different. Now, there is a divide between the kingdom of God and all other kingdoms. No action short of the literal return of Christ will make any earthly nation God's nation.

d) Nevertheless, God has placed every Christian in some nation or other, and we are required to seek good for our neighbors. The good of the nation as a whole includes its divinely ordained function to maintain justice for its citizens and its neighbors. Christians participate in this civic life out of love for their neighbor, but they do so as *aliens*. Christians are, first and foremost, citizens of another kingdom.

e) When the servants of Jesus refused to fight to keep him out of Pilate's hands, that made them weak and ineffectual according to Pilate's political realm. Yet the gospel triumphed. We must consider what it will look like today for Christians to enter politics in that way. The kingdoms of the world return evil for evil; they lie for profit, hide their weaknesses, and refuse to acknowledge when they are wrong. The nations of the world store up treasures for themselves on earth; they reward the proud, despise the lowly, and advertise their own good deeds. Disciples of Jesus must follow the command of our Lord to repudiate these things, and the wisdom of the world will condemn that kind of political participation to failure. But the wisdom of the world knows neither the wisdom of God nor the power of God. Our hope, and our work, as Christians (in politics and everywhere else) is for our neighbors to see what God is like, and see that the kingdom of God is not of this world, though it is the hope of this world.

So, this meditation is not so much about Christian political action or policy as it is about Christian *witness*. It has been said that witnessing is about giving knowledge, not telling people what to do.[1] That powerful insight applies to the aim of this book in two ways. First, as already noted, I won't try to tell you who to vote for, or what side to take in policy controversies. My aim is to remind us of what we know about Christ and his kingdom and to spell out a vision of that way, rooted in the gospel and dedicated to revealing it. You may find this disconcerting at times. It is often more comfortable to be told what to do than it is to be faced with challenging questions. But raising questions is my aim (maybe that's the philosopher in me, not just the Bible teacher). We must wrestle with the implications of the gospel for how we participate in the kingdoms of the world where we find ourselves scattered.

Those implications bring us to the second way in which this meditation embraces the idea of witness. "You will be my witnesses," said Jesus at his ascension, "to the ends of the earth." If that is more about revealing what we know than about telling people what to do, why has the distinctively Christian element of political action seemed so often to run toward telling people what to do? I think that we can actively and faithfully engage in politics as Christians without doing that—certainly without *legislating* that. That is the vision of Christian political life in the twenty-first century that I hope to stir up, because it reflects and exalts the gospel of Jesus Christ.

---

1 Dallas Willard, *Living in Christ's Presence: Final Words on Heaven and the Kingdom of God* (Downers Grove: IVP Books, 2014), 12.

Take this with you:

❖ The way the servants of Jesus fight is evidence for the kind of kingdom we profess to serve.

❖ The aim of this meditation is not to advocate for or against particular political policies or parties, but to identify biblical principles for Christian political participation that bears true witness to the gospel.

II.

Who made me a judge?

Someone in the crowd said to him, "Teacher, tell my brother to divide the inheritance with me." Jesus replied, "Man, who appointed me a judge or an arbiter between you?" Then he said to them, "Watch out! Be on your guard against all kinds of greed; life does not consist in an abundance of possessions."

(Luke 12:13–15).

A single incident in scripture does not give us a complete doctrine of political participation. But everything Jesus does (or refuses to do) tells us *something*—so let's (cautiously) explore this one. This incident provokes questions, and thinking them through shows us something important, which resonates throughout the Bible, about efforts to enlist Jesus for our side in political debates.

That's just what this man in the crowd was trying to do, isn't it? We don't know whether his brother was breaking the rules about inheritance, or whether this guy wanted the rules to change. We can charitably assume that he was making an appeal for justice as he saw it, but it won't affect our interpretation if, in fact, he just wanted some of what his brother had whether he had a right to it or not. What is Jesus's response? He refuses to intervene in the dispute, and goes so far as to challenge the petitioner by asking: "Who made me a judge or an arbiter between you?"

But wait—isn't Jesus the judge of all the earth? "We must all appear before the judgment seat of Christ," says Paul (and Matthew and Mark and John). And John writes, "Just as the Father has life in Himself, even so He gave to the Son also to have life in Himself; and He gave Him authority to execute judgment, because He is the Son of Man." (5:26–27) So, we know that it was God who made Jesus a judge, but that isn't what this exchange is about. Jesus's question here seems to be rhetorical, designed to say, "I'm not a judge or arbiter between you." Jesus plainly refuses that role here. The role he is refusing is not the final judgment of humanity, but of deciding "between" them in this case. *Jesus refuses to be an arbiter in this merely temporal political dispute.*

This is really important. The inheritance, whether shared or not, is a matter of this life—a temporal issue. When this man and his brother are dead, the actual division of the inheritance won't matter a bit to either of them—it'll be past history, its significance gone with their earthly life. There *is* something here that will matter eternally, but it isn't the details of who gets how much of the money. What matters eternally is the condition of their hearts, and Jesus does address that. "Watch out," he says, "Be on guard against greed." Then Jesus tells a story to remind this man—and all the onlookers—that what matters in life is not how much stuff we have. The story is a familiar one; it is the parable of the rich farmer who built extra barns, put his trust in them, and was branded a fool when death overtook him suddenly. We know the story, but maybe we haven't paid enough attention to the *context* of the story. Why does Jesus tell it here, after refusing to take sides about dividing the inheritance? The man must be approaching the dispute with his brother as if the most important thing in life really is how much stuff we have. What does it mean to think that way, and then try to get Jesus on your side? And if Jesus did take your side, what would that say about who he is? What would that say about the gospel? It would put Jesus on one side or another of a merely temporal dispute in a way that would implicate him in a scheme of values that is distorted, or just plain false.

Jesus refuses to take sides on disputes that concern only temporal affairs, on things that will not matter at the end of life. Many preachers have said that God does not come to take sides, but "to take over," and have quite rightly pointed out the relevance of this fact for Christians and politics.[2] But sometimes this insight gets turned around to imply that if we find out what God really intends then we can get on God's side, and that ends up being one side or another of the original dispute. What if God really is on NEITHER side of temporal disputes—including many of our political disputes? I think that this is often the case. In disputes that are entirely temporal, it may always be the case. This fact is illustrated by Jesus's stance here in Luke 12—he refuses to be a judge or arbiter—but the idea does not depend on this passage alone for support. It follows from the deepest truths in scripture about humanity.

We've seen Jesus refuse to take sides in a legal case about the distribution of money in an inheritance. We're asking: why would he refuse to be a judge or arbitrator in this situation? For a potential explanation, let's look at what a biblical account of humanity implies about the *tragic nature* of temporal politics.

Human beings are made in the image of God. Humanity is the crown of God's creative work, and people have infinite value—dignity beyond price. And yet, human beings are fallen, according to scripture. Humanity has joined a rebellion against God which has marred every person with corruption. These two facts are evident in human life and history. Are there any creatures on earth

---

2   for example, Tony Evans, *How Should Christians Vote?* (Chicago: Moody Publishers, 2012), 60.

capable of such nobility and beauty as humans? And, are there any creatures capable of such evil, depravity, and pain? The reality of life in our fallen world is reflected in this duality, this contradiction. Are humans good, or capable of good? Yes. Are we evil, or capable of evil? Yes. Humanity reflects, and individual humans reflect, *both* of these characteristics.

But as we think about our lives, or ways of organizing the lives of people around us, this contradictory nature disrupts our thinking. We tend to drift toward one characterization or another. We might do this in particular circumstances, or we might adopt a positive or a negative view of humanity in a more general way. But a one-sided view will always be inadequate, because the other pole is just as real—if what the scriptures teach us about humanity is true. In practice this means that *no temporal solutions to the problems of human life together are perfect*. In fact, since the decision between competing policies so often depends on emphasizing either the goodness or the corruption of humanity, this probably means that no political policy is completely good. Stop and think about that: what if no political policy can be completely good?

Let's take two current hot-button issues in the United States to illustrate: gun control and immigration. Don't worry, I'm not going to take sides—I'm in the middle of arguing that *Jesus* doesn't take a side. As policy questions, these issues each involve competing values[3]. Consider gun control. Conscientious people argue (correctly, in my view) that individual liberty is served when citizens, and not just the government, are armed, and the U.S. Constitution has some provision for protecting this liberty. It is also the case that innocent (and intrinsically valuable) people suffer and die in the United States because of the prevalence of firearms in the hands of people who have little regard for the lives of others.

---

3 The term "competing *goods*" is often used in this context; I'll use "values" because that sense of "goods" may seem weird to those who don't hang around philosophers. But I want to emphasize that I don't mean things that people happen to value or approve of, but things that are actually valuable in an objective sense, no matter what anyone thinks of them. These are cases where two things really are both good, and we have to choose one over the other.

Any policy which regulates who can have guns will balance the good of protecting people with the good of preserving liberty. No policy can fully promote both values at the same time—*and they are both good*. That makes every actual gun policy an enemy of some good or value—every one. Now that we are warmed up, think about immigration. What values require that nations regulate their borders? And, what values like human liberty, dignity, and physical well-being are threatened by policies regulating the borders of the United States and other nations?

Gun regulation and immigration are just two examples; consider the tension between freedom and protection in economic systems, in education, law enforcement, and so on. It seems that *any* actual policy will have tragic consequences; it will fail to achieve perfect good, because policies take positions which, in a broken world, must weigh or choose between competing values.

I'm not saying that you and I shouldn't take sides. We have a responsibility as citizens to help decide policies about guns, borders, and many other things. I'm saying that any particular policy we support will be imperfect—in the significant sense that our policy will diminish some valuable outcome *while promoting other values*. It will force us to choose in some way between values like liberty and safety, both of which are rooted in the dignity of people made in the image of God, and both of which are threatened by individual and collective human corruption. What policies would Jesus support if he were a U.S. citizen? I have no idea. But he isn't a U.S. citizen, and in at least one instructive case he refused to use his (vastly greater) authority to be a judge or arbiter about a temporal issue.

If Jesus declines the role of political arbiter, does that mean Jesus doesn't care? Not at all. In refusing to arbitrate he did not refuse to instruct. To the guy who wanted Jesus to take his side in the inheritance case he warned against greed, and against believing that possessions define life. The fool in Jesus's responding parable believed that the question of how to store his wealth—the temporal issue—was the only question that mattered. What if Christians in the United States approached questions of gun control, immigration, or economics as if life consisted entirely of temporal concerns? What if we tried to appeal to the authority of Jesus about temporal matters in a way that obscured or denied the tragic circumstances of humanity as both corrupt and infinitely valuable? This would be a great betrayal of our calling, our witness. But on the positive side, what might it look like for Christians in the United States to address these policy questions in light of the gospel, whatever side any of us might take?

Approaching policy questions in light of the gospel means taking the tragic nature of politics seriously. Because humans are fallen, every policy is going to end up allowing people to get hurt— sometimes causing them to get hurt. And because humans are made in the image of God, hurting them isn't trivial, and it isn't ok. (We're not just talking about humans hurting themselves, but being hurt *because of* the policy we establish, and every policy will in some way do that.) This doesn't mean there isn't a best policy, or a right policy, or a policy that everybody ought to adopt. It just means that even the best or right policy isn't perfect—it will diminish some good or undercut some value. Approaching policy questions in light of the gospel means acknowledging this tragic fact—even while we are advocating for a policy position on one side or the other.

Things would be easier, of course, if policy questions were simple affairs of good versus evil. Everybody knows that in a case like that, the position that is for the good and against the evil is the right choice. And so, naturally, that's the way we (and our political opponents) characterize our political policy disputes. "Those people oppose my policy because they are evil, and because they are trying to achieve some bad thing" is a very powerful argument—if it is true. And sometimes, maybe, it is. But it isn't always true. In fact, to suppose that some group of people is *always* wrong (and, therefore, another group … usually mine … is always right) is to deny the fallenness of humanity—and therefore unbiblical. The reason why so many policy questions are so hard to permanently resolve is that these disputes are not about good versus evil, they are about good versus good. Honesty demands that we acknowledge when policy disputes about temporal matters involve competing values, which means that neither position is perfectly good.

But wouldn't that be playing right into a political opponent's hands? They can say, "If we don't adopt my policy, this valuable thing will be lost." And the honest response is, "Yes, that is true, and that is bad." So, it *is* playing into a political opponent's hands in a way that is shockingly different from the normal politics of our time. But what else are Christians going to do, refuse to talk about policy in light of the gospel? Shall we pretend that one side is wholly good, and that's the side Jesus is on? The gospel doesn't tell us which side to take in a merely temporal policy matter. Instead, it reminds us of the brokenness of the world, the imperfection of human institutions, and our need for a savior. (The gospel also demands that we acknowledge the truth, even when that's painful to our pride and our ambitions.) On the positive side, even if talking about policy in light of the gospel makes Christians political misfits, it shows our neighbors something. It shows that Christians care about the good, and that they seem to be oriented toward something outside the temporal scheme of things. That is to say: it keeps the gospel visible and central in our lives and our testimony.

The centrality of the gospel in our political participation should free us from fear. How often does our culture, especially our political culture, say, "You can't do that!" (even about things like telling the truth)? They're afraid of losing, and they want you and me to be afraid too. But our hope is not in what Paul calls "the wisdom of this world," it is in the cross of Christ—which Paul admits is considered foolishness but actually reveals the power of God. This doesn't mean we like it—or that we should like it—when our carefully considered political policies fail to catch on. It just means that we understand the limitations of the temporal systems we live in, and that we have hope to offer that goes beyond them, even while we are working within them.

So, if temporal politics really are tragic, and Jesus really might not take sides on a particular political policy question, what are the implications? The first is straightforward: on such policy questions, there wouldn't be a "Christian" answer. There'd be answers that Christians give, but there would not be only one answer that all Christians are supposed to give in order to be on God's side. This does not mean that our commitment to Christ is irrelevant to our political decisions, and it doesn't mean that politics is outside the realm of faithful discipleship. But it does mean that Christian political decision-making is not as simple as just "taking God's side" on policy questions.

Figuring out which side God is on hasn't done much for Christianity or for politics anyway. Many Christians who some would call "liberal" have ended up identifying God's side as lining up with the most left-leaning political party available. And many "conservative" Christians have claimed that God's positions just happen to line up with the most right-leaning political party. Both groups take themselves to be putting commitment to God above politics, but we have good reason to think that politics really has the top priority. If we are honest, we must admit that each group has to ignore some biblical concerns or principles in order to keep God always on the side of one party or the other. And we end up grouped by that part of God's revelation which just happens to align with one particular political ideology or another, rather than by commitment to the whole counsel of God. This shows that politics, not scripture, is in the driver's seat. Recognizing the tragic and limited nature of temporal politics will liberate us from this worldly bondage.

Let's be clear: there is no place for compromise of our theological convictions, no place for compromise of biblical principles. But the realm of politics is the realm of compromise; it must be: the congress or the city council is *everybody's* government, and to function effectively they must craft policies that take account of competing political ideologies. The view that God takes sides on policy means the end of political compromise, because political compromise would be theological compromise. If that were the case, then Christians would either have to totally separate ourselves from politics, or totally control the political system. Total control is not biblical, as we will see in the course of this meditation. Should we totally abandon politics? That would be better than compromising the gospel, but my point here is that Christians are free to participate in the political order, with its compromises, while maintaining the uncompromised integrity of our biblical principles. That liberation comes from the realization that God does not take sides on every temporal policy question.

Let me say a little more about the troubling question of compromise—especially moral compromise. Remember that most policy decisions involve competing goods: increasing liberty decreases equality (and vice versa), and both liberty and equality are good. Freedom and protection is another common set of competing values (we experience that tension every time we go through security to get on an airplane). Every policy prioritizes some good over others, and most policy disagreements are about which value should carry the most weight in a particular kind of case. Every policy is imperfect because it diminishes some good or another. But, surely there are limits: some things are so valuable, or some other things are so trivial, or the amount of one good obtained is so small compared to how much of another good is lost that a particular policy decision must be morally ruled out. I do not deny this, and I am not advocating moral compromise in the name of political compromise. This is messy, of course, because we do not all agree about where the moral line should be drawn. Morally sensitive and responsible people might disagree, even faithful Bible-believing Christians might disagree. I am not saying that politics is the realm where Christians (or anybody else) may do evil in order that good should come. I am not advocating that we violate our conscience. But I *am* saying that sometimes we must support policies that we recognize are not wholly good—or else we must get out of politics—because of the tragic nature of our broken humanity.

We are never to be careless or cavalier about valuable things that are lost because of our actions. This means that Christian participation in tragic politics is a path of grief. If we follow our Lord in recognizing eternal values, we will grieve when we fall short of them—even if this shortcoming is inevitable in the tragic circumstances of policy-making in a broken world. This realization changes the *attitude* with which we participate in temporal politics, whatever policy positions we are bound by conscience and reflection to take.

Why emphasize attitude over policy position? For one thing, it is honest about the complexity—and the tragedy—of political policy. But does attitude really make a difference? I think it makes a lot of difference. Consider this: we rightly fear to be found opposing God and, naturally, our emotions are aroused when we encounter others opposing God. Recognizing that God may not take sides on merely temporal political policies provides us some emotional distance from the political disagreements we engage in.[4] This not only changes our tone, but enables us to listen more carefully, respond more charitably, and recognize significant points made by our opponents as well as to acknowledge the valuable things they may be seeking. Emotional distance is not always good, but consider how rare these conversational characteristics seem to be in political debate these days. Christians who display them fulfill the admonition to "show yourself an example of those who believe in speech, conduct, love, faith, and purity," and to "let your speech always be with grace, as though seasoned with salt."

---

4 Jamie Smith's delightful phrase "sanctified ambivalence" captures this idea perfectly. See the opening story in the introduction to *Awaiting the King: Reforming Public Theology* (Grand Rapids, MI: Baker Academic, 2017), p. 3.

Jesus was in some sense *above* temporal disagreements around
him. It's not that he didn't care, and he certainly wasn't arrogant,
condescending, or disdainful. He just had them in perspective. He
looked at everyday squabbles from the perspective of eternity; that
perspective includes the weight of moral considerations and attitudes
in contrast to self-interest (That perspective also includes the inevitable
end of the present system of the world.). In counseling that we
adopt some form of his aloofness from temporal squabbles, I want
to emphasize that disciples should cultivate this sensitivity to eternal
things. Remember that, although Jesus refused to take sides in the
disagreement about inheritance, he immediately addressed the deeper
issue: "Be on your guard against all kinds of greed." What would it
look like for us to follow his example? It's a little weird because we are
in temporal disagreements; we are participants in political decisions in
a way that Jesus is not, and we do have a responsibility to take sides
in many cases. But suppose that instead of emphasizing that God is
on the side of our particular policy, we acknowledge our aim to be on
God's side of bigger questions. God cares about freedom. God cares
about justice. God cares about greed, and cruelty. God cares about
those who are broken and powerless. God cares about the innocent.
Christians can and should affirm these truths, using whatever
language we think most effective. But, given the tragic nature of
politics in a fallen world, these principles alone may not tell us which
specific policy to adopt. Let us, then, offer our policy views in humility,
with a certain sort of aloofness, since, unlike the Word of God, political
policies will be imperfect *even when they are right.*

> *"And [Jesus] said to His disciples, 'For this reason I say
> to you, do not worry about your life, as to what you will
> eat; nor for your body, as to what you will put on. For
> life is more than food, and the body more than clothing.'"*
>
> (Luke 12:22–23).

It is no accident that, in Luke 12, Jesus turns and gives this
admonition to his disciples immediately after the events we have

been discussing. To review: a man comes and asks Jesus to resolve a dispute with his brother about inheritance; Jesus refuses to take sides in the dispute and proceeds to warn the man against greed with a parable about the folly of thinking that life consists of material things. Then he turns to his disciples and tells them not to worry about the merely temporal conditions of life. These verses will also be familiar from the sermon on the mount. "Consider the lilies," Jesus memorably says, "consider the birds of the air." What is the point? Don't worry about clothes, food, drink—temporal conditions of life. What should we do instead? *Seek first the kingdom of God and His righteousness, and all these things will be added to you."*

This is the attitude which must inform our political participation. The kingdom of God is not of this world; that's what Jesus is proclaiming when he admonishes the hearers to righteousness rather than taking sides in merely temporal disputes. To the unbeliever, a warning: "Be on your guard against greed." To the disciple, an encouragement: "Do not be afraid, little flock, for your Father has chosen gladly to give you the kingdom." He does not promise an earthly kingdom, one of food, drink, and clothing; and that's what temporal politics is about—along with protecting the innocent from evil. When Jesus concludes by telling the disciples to get purses that will not wear out, a treasure in heaven that will not fail, he is counseling them to get on his side. That means caring more about the righteousness of God's kingdom than about *either side* of a temporal policy decision.

Still, we are in earthly kingdoms, and our neighbors are affected for better and worse by political policies that we may have a hand in deciding. If Jesus doesn't take sides on details of the governance of earthly kingdoms, does he tell us how to do it? Let's begin to tackle these issues with a historical detour, back to the fourth century, when Christians and the church began a new era of political participation in the Roman Empire.

Take this with you:

❖ Politics is tragic in a fallen world: every political policy achieves some good at the expense of other goods. So no political policy can be completely good.

❖ Christian political decision-making is not as simple as just "taking God's side" on policy questions.

❖ Seeking the kingdom of God first means pursuing eternal values, and recognizing that no particular political policy fully serves them—even those policies which we support on the basis of conscience.

III.

Lessons from St. Augustine

While he was in custody awaiting transfer to Rome, the apostle Paul was questioned by King Agrippa. The interview, reported in Acts 26, proved to be an opportunity for Paul to give his testimony and preach the gospel to the king. In the end, Agrippa famously said to Paul, "Soon you will persuade me to become a Christian." Think about that. What if he *had* become a Christian? The text doesn't tell us what might have followed, or should have followed, from the king's conversion. In fact, the New Testament doesn't have much at all to say about Christians holding positions in temporal governments.

The gospels and the epistles don't tell us how cheek-turning, putting-away-the-sword, my-kingdom-is-not-of-this-world living is possible while *bearing* the sword of the state *in* this world. That could be because it really isn't possible (an option that we must take seriously), but it also could be because those were not the issues of New Testament times. Our "what if" question about King Agrippa is just a fantastical speculation. Prior to the fourth century, Christianity was sometimes tolerated and sometimes persecuted, but for the followers of Jesus *governing* was simply not an option.

But in AD 313, the emperor Constantine ended religious persecution with the Edict of Toleration. (Whether Constantine himself was really a believer is something we don't know, but without question the social and political profile of Christianity was rising during his reign.) By 381, under the emperor Theodosius, Christianity had become the official religion of the empire. Now Christians had to face the question of how disciples of Jesus might take up the sword as members of the civil government. As things turned out, some think they never should have done it. But Augustine, Bishop of Hippo, in North Africa, showed a way of doing it that clearly extended the teaching of the gospels and the epistles. Ironically, Augustine may also have been responsible—at least in part—for the later excesses of the imperial church in the Middle Ages which seemed in so many ways to have forgotten the gospel. These are the lessons, good and bad, that we can learn from St. Augustine.

So let's flash back in time to the end of the fourth century, and use a brief analysis of Augustine's thought and the times he lived in to help us think about our own times, the issues we face, and the responsibilities we bear. We'll organize our exploration around these five questions:

1. Who is Augustine, and what is the background of his teaching about Christians and government?

2. How can followers of Jesus's teaching be part of earthly governments that live by the sword?

3. If Christians are part of the government, should they make laws promoting the faith?

4. In spite of his teaching, why is Augustine thought to be "the father of the inquisition"?

5. How does religious legislation hide or misrepresent the gospel?

Who is Augustine, and what is the background of his teaching about Christians and government?

Augustine was born in North Africa and, well into a career as a philosopher and Roman teacher of rhetoric, he converted to Christianity in AD 386, at the age of thirty-one. He was soon ordained a priest and by 395 was Bishop of the city of Hippo in North Africa. He went on to become one of the most influential theologians of the church.

The most important biblical idea which Augustine uses to guide political participation is this: Christians are, first and foremost, members of a society that cuts across all earthly governments and institutions. Not even the church (as a temporal organization) defines Christians, who are members of what Augustine calls the "City of God." This "city" is not a political entity, but one of two spiritual categories into which all humanity is divided without remainder. In his greatest work, *The City of God*, Augustine explains it this way:

> For all the difference of the many and very great nations throughout the world in religion and morals, language, weapons and dress, there exist no more than two kinds of society, which, according to our Scriptures, we have rightly called the two cities. One city is that of men who live according to the flesh. The other is of men who live according to the spirit. (Book 14: Chapter 1)

These aren't earthly "societies," but spiritual categories; membership in these communities is not determined by institutional affiliation, nor any other external sign, but by *loving* and *willing*. Members of the earthly city ("the City of Man") are characterized by love of themselves and their own ends, and by enmity towards the will of God. The "City of God" consists of those who love and honor God. We can put it this way: the City of God is all true Christians from all times and places.

> What we see, then, is that two societies have issued from two kinds of love. Worldly society has flowered from a selfish love which dared to despise even God, whereas the communion of the saints is rooted in a love of God that is ready to trample on self (14:28).

These opposing spiritual communities transcend all human institutions. No earthly organization consists exclusively of one city's members. Augustine recognizes that even the institutional church (all of whose members claim to be members of the City of God) is composed of a *mixture* of individuals from the two societies. Even though the focus of the church, as an institution, is God-centered and eternal, the "City of God" is not the Church. And, even though the focus of the state is largely temporal and practical, the "City of Man" is not the state or government. It is important to see that the essential enmity of the two cities does not represent a necessary conflict of earthly institutions like church and state. That opens the way for a principled account of Christian participation in civil government.

How can followers of Jesus's teaching be part of earthly governments that live by the sword?

The clear distinction between the spiritual societies and the temporal institutions of church and state provides grounds for uncompromised Christian participation in government. The key conceptual foundation for our participation is Augustine's notion of "common cause." Members of the earthly city *and* the heavenly require temporal peace secured by civil government. This common interest in civil order legitimizes the cooperation of Christians with their spiritual counterparts in the task of government. Augustine puts it this way:

> [T]he earthly city ... seeks only an earthly peace, and limits the goal of its peace, of its harmony of authority and obedience among its citizens, to the voluntary and collective attainment of objectives necessary to mortal existence. The heavenly City, meanwhile—or, rather, that part that is on pilgrimage in mortal life— ... must use this earthly peace until such time as our mortality which needs such peace has passed away ... [The heavenly City] has no hesitation about keeping in step with the civil law which governs matters pertaining to our existence here below. For, as mortal life is the same for all, there ought to be common cause between the two cities in what concerns our purely human living (19:17).

Affairs of the mortal life are organized and governed by civil authorities. Members of both spiritual cities have common interests regarding these affairs. The fact that Christians share those interests, combined with their abilities, and love for their neighbors, justifies (and maybe sometimes requires) Christian participation in civil government. This was happening in Augustine's time, and it happens now.

The basic picture is this: people who love God participate in the worship of God and Christian discipleship; they are part of an institution which organizes and enables that: the church. Those who are not Christians have no such interests and no part in the church. But Christians also need sewers, water, roads, protection from assault, etc., and these interests we have in common with all our neighbors—that's "common cause." Participation in institutions which organize and protect these temporal human needs (government or the state) serves our own interests *and* the needs of our neighbors. Given those needs, love for our neighbors would seem to require our stepping up to help meet them if we have the abilities and opportunities, and if it involves no compromise of our submission to God. With these principles, Augustine addresses the circumstances of Christians in the late Roman Empire from the perspective of the gospels and apostolic teaching.

If Christians are part of the government, should they make laws promoting the faith?

By the time Augustine becomes Bishop of Hippo, there are professing Christian emperors. If these rulers truly are members of the City of God, then another question arises: "Since Jesus followers *are* in government, shouldn't they use that power to get other people to become followers?" This is the question of religious legislation. Augustine opposes anti-religious (that is, anti-Christian) legislation. But, what about legislation *favoring* Christianity? If individual Christians are to spread their faith using all available means, what responsibilities fall to those who have the power of the state at their disposal? Are Christian rulers permitted, or required, to enact laws promoting Christianity?

Augustine's account of the nature of the two cities means that we must answer "no" to this question. That's because of the nature of civil government and of the heavenly city. Remember that, according to Paul, the government is "a minister of God, an avenger who brings wrath on the one who practices evil," and "it does not bear the sword for nothing" (Rom. 13). It bears the sword—the fundamental method that the state uses to accomplish its purpose is coercion, or force. But the defining features of the two cities, loving and willing, are not subject to coercion. Civil authority can regulate the external activities of individuals, but is powerless to force or prevent true participation in either the City of God or the earthly city. You can force people to do things or not do things, but you can't force them to love or not love things—and you can't force people to *freely* choose them.

Augustine acknowledges this limitation when he says that "men are not to be called good because they refrain from wrong-doing through the fear of [the power of kings]—no one is good through dread of punishment but through love of righteousness..." (Letter 153). Since the state can produce right action but not love, and the City of God is defined by "love of righteousness," not merely right actions, Christian rulers have no duty to enact legislation to produce the City of God. In fact, it seems that the opposite is true; since such efforts would *misrepresent* the nature of true religion, they ought to be avoided by Christian rulers. So, some kind of state religious neutrality seems to be dictated by the limitations of civil power and by Augustine's account (which I think is the biblical account) of the true nature of the people of God.

These claims, by the way, overlap the arguments of John Locke regarding religious legislation, a fact of interest to American readers since Locke is the direct source for many of Jefferson's ideas expressed in the Declaration of Independence and beyond. Locke's "Letter Concerning Toleration" (1689) affirms that those who would force assent to doctrine or religious practice cannot be advancing true religion. "The commonwealth," says Locke, "seems to me to be a society of men constituted only for the procuring, preserving, and advancing of their own civil interests ... The care of souls cannot belong to the civil magistrate because his power consists only in outward force; but true and saving religion consists in the inward persuasion of the mind, without which nothing can be acceptable to God."[5]

---

5   John Locke, *A Letter Concerning Toleration* (Indianapolis: Hackett Publishing Company, Inc., 1983) pp. 26-27.

In spite of his teaching, why is Augustine thought to be "the father of the inquisition"?

In spite of Locke's principles being clearly Augustinian, things were more complicated for the Bishop of Hippo. Even while he was writing *The City of God*, Augustine said (about the biblical command to work good to all people): "Let those who can do so achieve it by their sermons as Catholic preachers; let others who can do so achieve it by their laws as Catholic rulers." In this context, Augustine explicitly claims that kings "serve the Lord by enacting laws in favor of religion and against irreligion." (Letter 185, written in 417 AD). This seems to conflict with his account of the City of God. But we do not have to automatically assume that Augustine was being inconsistent (just as in our own time it may not be inconsistent for Christian political activists to push for godly rulers who will legislate according to biblical principle while explicitly denying that they favor "theocracy"). But even if these claims are not inconsistent, they do require an explanation. Let's look more closely at Augustine's thinking and action to find one. Probably the clearest place to look is his response to the Donatist controversy, in which he came finally to support imperial legislation to suppress heresy and preserve the unity of the church.

I don't want to oversimplify Augustine's circumstances regarding issues of church and state, or make them seem like modern circumstances. Bishops were already a part of the Roman legal system after 318; citizens could voluntarily have lawsuits transferred from civil courts to episcopal tribunals. From the point of view of Augustine's political theology, this seems to fall under the notion of common cause and love for neighbor—and, in fact, reflects Paul's declaration (I Corinthians 6) that Christians should be the most qualified to judge such cases fairly. But in the case of the Donatists, Augustine eventually went beyond enforcing secular laws (such as those against fraud, theft, and violence), and came to support legislation promoting orthodox Christian doctrine.

Donatism involved a controversy about the role in the church of bishops who had denied their faith under the persecutions of emperor Diocletian in 303–304. The faction which came to be named after Donatus—a North African bishop who was zealous for the purity of the church—aimed to restrict the acceptance of compromised bishops. But official church doctrine from Rome accepted the bishops and branded the Donatists as schismatic and heretical. This doctrinal dispute was made worse by cultural and political tensions between Rome and Africa, and political violence often erupted in the mix.

The controversy was still raging between Catholics and Donatists when Augustine became a bishop in North Africa. From the beginning, Augustine favored legislation against the terrorist violence—this was just an application of secular law. But, though he publicly opposed Donatist doctrines, Augustine did not initially favor state intervention on the doctrinal dispute or the question of church unity. We see this in his letter to a Donatist bishop in 392:

> I shall not take any action while the army is present, lest anyone of yours should think that I wanted to use force rather than a peaceful method ... I shall see to it that all who hear us may know that it was no part of my plan that men should be forced into any communion against their will, but that truth should be manifest to those seeking it in quietness (Letter 23).

Augustine continued to oppose state intervention in the doctrinal dispute. Around the turn of the century he wrote, "I am displeased that schismatics are violently coerced to communion by the force of any secular power." Such disagreements, he affirmed, were to be resolved by appeal to the Word of God, and disagreements about interpretation of the scriptures resolved by study, rational argument, and discernment about tradition. Later, however, Augustine changed his mind.

By 408, we see Augustine explaining his reversal of opinion about imperial religious legislation:

> [M]y first feeling about it was that no one was to be forced into the unity of Christ, but that we should act by speaking, fight by debating, and prevail by our reasoning, for fear of making pretended Catholics out of those whom we knew as open heretics. But this opinion of mine has been set aside, not because of opposing arguments, but by reason of proved facts (Letter 93).

What were these "proved facts"? Apparently, they were large numbers of converts from Donatism to mainstream Catholicism which resulted from the imperial decrees. But Augustine claimed that he never abandoned the principle that righteousness and true religion cannot be coerced; he denied that anyone had been forced into genuine faith. Instead he said that the laws stirred many from complacency, forced them to reconsider the issues, and offered them protection—thus opening the way for a sincere conversion. At one point, he describes such conversions as "conquests of the Lord" and the laws facilitating them as the actions of shepherds gathering "wandering sheep of Christ."

Let's accept Augustine's claim that in supporting this legislation he did not deny the essential divide between the City of God and coercive earthly government. A close reading of his arguments supports his assertion, but more importantly for our purposes, accepting his claim enables us to see the true implications—and dangers—of his strategy. Augustine knew that we can't build the kingdom of God with force—his teaching on this is clear (and biblical). But he came to think that it was possible to build the *church*—though not the heavenly city—via temporal force. People can, after all, be forced to go to church, or to stop proclaiming heretical doctrines, even though they cannot be forced to truly believe. Augustine thought that imperial legislation could smooth the path for Donatist conversion by removing excuses for separation, suppressing political violence which clouded the doctrinal issues, and generally providing positive influence and encouragement toward orthodox belief.

The impact of this policy goes far beyond the immediate issue of the Donatist schism in North Africa; we can say without exaggeration that the history of the Church was affected for centuries by its dependence upon imperial power. The church spread with the empire, and aligned its power with the sword. And everything that Augustine admitted he feared from such an alliance came to pass: a politically powerful church which brought in people because of worldly interests rather than faith; pastors more interested in power, wealth, and honor than religious duty; distraction of church leaders by political and economic interest. Augustine's support of specifically religious legislation gives credence to those who have called him the "Father of the Inquisition."

How does religious legislation hide or misrepresent the gospel?

In trying to save souls by using the sword (state coercion), Augustine supported church policies which tragically and fatally misrepresented the true nature of the kingdom of God. To see this, think about his Donatist opponents: *they* knew that salvation lay in the transformation of what the soul loves and wills, and force cannot accomplish this. So, when faced with a church threatening them with imperial punishment to conform, they can only see that as a form of corruption. They know, as Augustine knows, that the true gospel of the kingdom is a matter of loving and willing. They are bound by conscience to be persuaded by biblical argument, not fear of the sword (Consider Peter and John in Acts 4:19.). The message that comes on the point of a sword or at the end of a gun *can't* be seen as the true gospel of Jesus Christ—even if, due to misguided zeal, it aims to present the message of Christ.

The tragedy in all this is not about Augustine's reputation, but about the way in which aligning the church and its methods with the kingdoms of this world hides the gospel of Jesus Christ. This should concern us in our own day, because we are so often led down these same paths by the pressing concerns around us. In the United States, those concerns and the related legislation are not directly doctrinal, like the anti-Donatist laws, or laws about who can take holy communion or what it means. What is more common are theologically inspired legal restrictions on everyday activity, like what used to be called "blue laws." But when the only justification for such laws is theological, they, too, run the risk of misrepresenting the gospel. Let's look at that more closely.

It certainly seems to be the case that legal restriction of commerce on Sundays, because it's Sunday, is an example of legislation whose justification is theological. (I'm selecting the example of blue laws because they are familiar to many American readers, but not an issue of great current controversy.) Let's suppose that it really is God-honoring to avoid selling unnecessary goods, or cars, or beer, on Sundays. For the sake of the illustration, let's also suppose that God requires that we avoid this commerce on Sunday. There are, of course, plenty of other things that God requires us to not do— murder, for example. But we don't have to appeal to God in order to justify laws against murder; we can talk about the equal value of persons, or equal rights. But for laws about selling on Sunday, we have to talk about God to defend the law. That's what I mean by a theological law. How do theological laws misrepresent the gospel?

Such laws do not necessarily misrepresent God. (Remember we are assuming for the sake of the illustration that God really doesn't want people to sell on Sunday because it fails to honor God.) It would be fine for me as a Christian to say that nobody should sell

on Sunday, and I'd almost certainly have the chance to say that
when people ask me why I don't do it. But what happens when
we make it a law? We are then saying to our unbelieving neighbors
that they must act as if they honor God *when they do not even believe
in God*. Even if they are temporarily better off for it (everybody
needs a break from work), are they eternally better off? Have they
been reconciled to God by being required to act as if they believe in
God? No—not any more so than if they had been required by law
to go to church. Further, and even more damaging, relationship to
God is represented to them as outward conformity to enforceable
rules. That's not the gospel of Jesus Christ; it is the belief of the
religious leaders who agitated to have Jesus killed. What irony and
what tragedy if, while seeking to honor God, we represent the path
to God as empty Phariseeism!

Let me emphasize two things about this illustration. First, I am
affirming that it is quite possible for it to be true that something
is wrong or offensive to God and yet false that we should try to
make it illegal. But, how can a person faithfully say God opposes
something and at the same time advocate for allowing it? The
answer is my second point.

This illustration leads us to the significance of *conscience*: the
importance of leaving people as free as possible to pursue their
own convictions about what is right—even if they are mistaken
about what is right. We do this because we take humanity
seriously, following God who left Adam and Eve free to do what
was forbidden. We do this because in proclaiming the gospel of
Jesus Christ we do not present *ourselves* as demanding repentance.
Our unbelieving neighbors face the wrath of God, but they do not
face *our* wrath. We must never obscure that fact, and so, we must
never enforce the Word of God with the sword of the state. We say
to our neighbors, you are free to spurn God, but you will answer
to God. The kingdom of God is not of this world, and *we must not
give the false impression that it is*.

And so Augustine stands as our teacher and our example. His theology of the two cities tells us why the gospel cannot be spread by the sword, and it also tells us how—out of love for neighbor and common cause in temporal matters—Christians might faithfully participate in the governments of this world. But his example also warns us: even if we think that we can use the sword of earthly kingdoms to push people toward the kingdom of God while technically keeping these kingdoms distinct, we should not—we must not. When Jesus commanded, "Do not fear those who kill the body but are unable to kill the soul, but rather fear Him who is able to destroy both soul and body in hell," he was telling us about the nature of God, the nature of the world, and the nature of salvation. Our primary obligation as Christians is to faithfully represent that to the nations. We dare not let our participation in civil government obscure the true nature of the gospel—these are the lessons from St. Augustine.

Take this with you:

❖ Christians share common interests with all people—including the concern for peace and order which good government exists to promote. This "common cause," along with love for neighbor, is a basis for Christian participation in civil government.

❖ Christian rulers have no duty to enact legislation to produce the City of God, because the law works by coercion, and true Christian faith cannot be coerced.

❖ Not everything that is offensive to God should be illegal.

A Nation for God

*Now these things happened to them as an example, and
they were written for our instruction, upon whom the
ends of the ages have come.*

(I Cor 10:11).

We've used Augustine to introduce an invitation and a warning.
The invitation is for Christians to participate in the divinely ordained
work of social organization and civil government. The warning is
against doing this in a way which obscures the true nature of the
gospel and the kingdom of God, as religious legislation seems to do.
In the next chapter, I will offer a model of civic participation which
is biblical and clearly reflects the gospel. But first, let's consider
a possible objection to my claims so far: the nation of Israel under
the law of Moses. Isn't this a model for a God-ordained and God-
honoring legal system? Does it show that my resistance to religious
legislation is wrong? I don't think so. In fact, the opposite is true:
the example of Israel under what Christians call the "old covenant"
is an important part of the argument *against* theological legislation.
The old covenant is aimed at the new in a way that affirms what we
have said so far about government and the gospel.

Old Testament Israel is not a model for a Christian nation—in fact,
it is a warning against the possibility of a Christian nation. This

doesn't mean that we throw out the Old Testament, or that the law and the prophets don't apply right now to our theology and our lives. But we must never forget that, in the purposes of God, the old covenant—and the nation of Israel—is the root and foundation of the new covenant in Jesus Christ, and of a people of God from every nation, tongue, and tribe. Let's review that history and those purposes.

The rise and fall (and fulfillment) of Israel under the law of Moses begins with God's promise to Abraham that through his descendants all the people of the earth would be blessed (Genesis 12:3[6]). The story unfolds in the next generations through Abraham's children, grandchildren, and great-grandchildren, who were people like you and me. That is, they had talents and weaknesses; they were fearful and selfish and sometimes did the right thing; they sometimes ignored and sometimes dimly trusted the promises of God—who was often silent, yet sometimes burst into their lives. The Bible's account of the patriarchs ends with Abraham's great-grandson Joseph in Egypt with his family and his eleven brothers and their families. They would become "the twelve tribes of Israel" when—four hundred years later—their descendants left Egypt to return to the land which they understood God promised to Abraham's people.

Moses, of course, was the leader of this multitude as they left Egypt, and it was to Moses that God's law was revealed at Sinai. The law represents the covenant God has made with this people as a nation. In the book of Deuteronomy, Moses declares:

> For what great nation is there that has a god so near
> to it as is the Lord our God whenever we call on Him?
> Or what great nation is there that has statutes and
> judgments as righteous as this whole law which I am
> setting before you today? (Deuteronomy 4:7–8).

---

6   and 22:18, 26:4, 28:14, Acts 3:25, Galatians 3:8

Under the covenant, defined by the law of Moses, the chosen people of God were a *nation*—an earthly kingdom. True, it wasn't like other nations (at least, it wasn't supposed to be); that's the point of it being "chosen." But the people of God were *nationally* defined. The law of Moses included moral principles, guidelines for worship and atonement for sin, distinctive cultural rules, and civil regulations for the ordering of day-to-day life. All of these were combined in a legal system with civil and criminal penalties ranging from fines to capital punishment. The law of Moses governed the whole of life for citizens of the chosen nation of God. But this proved to be a yoke that the people of Israel were not able to bear (to use the words of Peter in Acts 15). For those of us who care about the Bible and the purposes of God, that ought to raise some questions: Why didn't this work? Did God make a mistake in setting things up this way? Why did the arrangement end? How is the gospel of Jesus Christ somehow the fulfillment of this sad history?

Those aren't all the possible questions, of course, and they probably aren't all of your questions. But, if we can see biblical answers for these questions, we will see how the old covenant reflects the gospel in pointing to the new, and understand how the law of Moses might speak to us without a nation for God.

The church's first martyr—a Jewish believer named Stephen—gave perhaps the clearest and most succinct analysis of the Israelites' failure to keep the covenant of Moses. Speaking to his persecutors, Stephen said:

> You men who are stiff-necked and uncircumcised in heart and ears are always resisting the Holy Spirit; you are doing just as your fathers did. Which one of the prophets did your fathers not persecute? They killed those who had previously announced the coming of the Righteous One, whose betrayers and murderers you have now become; you who received the law as ordained by angels, and yet did not keep it (Acts 7:51–53).

The story of the nation of Israel is the story of a covenant broken time and again. When Moses set forth the covenant and reviewed the law in Deuteronomy, he said that he was setting before the people and their descendants "a blessing and a curse." Blessing, if the law was followed, and curse, when it was not. Disobedience—with its consequence—began almost immediately, and set the pattern for the nation that bore the banner of being God's nation.

Stephen puts his finger on the key element when he calls the Israelites of his time "uncircumcised in heart." Their identity with God was defined externally—geographically, ethnically, and by imposed laws—but their *hearts* were no different than the people of all nations. And like us all, they followed their hearts.

We do not need to rehearse in detail the long and tragic history of Israel under the covenant of Moses, as recounted in the Hebrew Bible. Stephen's summary suffices. But let us note several themes. One is the righteousness of God. The law of Moses reflects this, and what it means for humans to emulate it—economically and sexually, in speech, fidelity, and character. Provision was made for moral failure, including repentance, restitution, and blood sacrifice. And yet the people allowed their selfish desires to rule them, and made a mockery of the means by which God invited them to seek reconciliation.

Another theme is the jealousy of God and the separateness of Israel as a nation belonging to God. God's jealousy is revealed in the absolute prohibition of service or worship to other gods. And Israel's separation was ensured not just by strong geographical identification with the land, but by a series of laws guaranteeing cultural distinction—concerning food, dress, marriage, worship, and art—which prevent the easy mixing of this people with the nations and cultures around them. It was through this people, defined and demarcated nationally and culturally, that God's promise to Abraham would be fulfilled. And yet these laws were ignored, scorned, and distorted. Prophets brought the accusation of lawlessness and the call to repentance from God. Sometimes they were heeded, sometimes not.

The cycle of disobedience, rebuke, restoration, and further disobedience accelerated to the point where the large northern part of the nation (which had become divided into the kingdoms of *Israel* and *Judah* soon after the peak of its national glory) was destroyed forever by the Assyrian Empire. The ten tribes of the northern kingdom were never again a nation, though the diminished kingdom of Judah—and the promise of God—endured. Later Judah was also ravaged by a great empire, Babylon, but not permanently destroyed. This remnant of the nation was uprooted from the land and taken into Babylonian captivity. The prophets said this was the judgment of God, according to the word of Moses that the nation would be blessed if they obeyed the law, and cursed if not. But the prophets also promised deliverance from Babylon, which did come to pass, restoring the nation—diminished but enduring in the purpose of God.

Throughout this history, and continuing through the long prophetic silence until John the Baptist arose during the Roman occupation and domination of Israel, God called this nation his chosen people (Maybe we should say: God called his chosen people this nation.). But though Israel was providentially preserved by God, the nation received as much of the curse foretold by Moses as it did the blessing. Why didn't it work? Stephen said it best: because the people were "stiff-necked," "uncircumcised in heart and ears," and "always resisting the Holy Spirit." Let's stop and think about that, because it is the central lesson. We have already seen that governments exercise their role by external force; laws dictate actions and enforce those demands by punishment. This is true of the law of Moses and the system (including civil government) that it ordered. *But the law of Moses did not change the hearts of the people of Israel.*

Consider the Word of God through Isaiah the prophet: "This people draw near with their words and honor me with their lip service, but they remove their hearts far from me, and their reverence for me consists of tradition learned by rote" (Isa. 29:13). Everything about living up to the covenant here is outward: words, promises, tradition that is followed but not understood. Centuries later, Jesus cites this very passage in proclaiming that the heart is the center of purity and devotion to God. The actions that the law governs, he warns, arise from the heart: "For out of the heart come evil thoughts, murders, adulteries, fornications, thefts, false witness, slanders." (Matt. 15:19) If the heart is not changed, the law cannot be kept. *And the law cannot change people's hearts.* So this nation for God, formed and ordered by a covenant of law, failed.

Did God make a mistake in setting things up this way? Obviously not, since God doesn't make mistakes. What we are really asking is why God would set things up so that the nation was doomed to fail because of the nature of law and of human sinfulness. We cannot always answer questions about why God does what God does, but in this case the scriptures give us at least some indication. In short: it was to demonstrate the gospel which is revealed in Jesus Christ.

I said before that the old covenant is aimed at the new, and this is precisely where we see that. In the midst of the nation's downfall, rife with apostasy and unrighteousness, suffering exile and captivity, the prophet Jeremiah proclaims:

> "Behold, days are coming," declares the Lord, "when I will make a new covenant with the house of Israel and with the house of Judah, not like the covenant which I made with their fathers in the day I took them by the hand to bring them out of the land of Egypt, My covenant which they broke, although I was a husband to them," declares the Lord. "But this is the covenant which I will make with the house of Israel after those days," declares the Lord, "I will put My law within them and on their heart I will write it; and I will be their God, and they shall be My people." (Jeremiah 31:31–34).

The covenant of law, broken in spite of God's faithful providence, is to be replaced by a new one. The new covenant has the law, but it is written *within* the people of God, not imposed upon them from the outside. The law of God is to be written on the hearts of his people. Do you see that this directly addresses the key element of the failure? Under the covenant of Moses, the people were identified with God by outward things, but their *hearts* were far from God; the new covenant changes this.

This is of course the very message that Jesus proclaims, and it is the apostolic teaching upon which the new covenant community is founded. Paul writes in Galatians that, "if a law had been given which was able to impart life, then righteousness would indeed have been based on law" (Gal. 3:21). Everyone who is bound by sin, says Paul, is also bound by law; "held in custody" is his description. That's why he calls the law "our tutor" (Gal. 3:24). The purpose of this tutor is "to lead us to Christ." Human slavery to sin—a condition of the heart—is revealed by the inability to keep the law. This is demonstrated in the fact that even the chosen people of God, when nationally and culturally defined by a regime of external law, cannot fulfill the requirements of the law—requirements, let's remember, that reflect the unchanging holiness and righteousness of God. And the inability of humans in their fallen condition to fulfill the law shows our need of a savior. The old covenant aims at the new; it serves the new; it demands the new.

Isn't that a pretty roundabout way for God's plan of salvation to unfold? Does it relegate centuries of history and generations of Jewish struggle to being mere instruments, pawns in the unfolding of the gospel of Jesus? No, and let me pause to be clear about a couple of points and qualifications. First, I write as a Christian to Christians, and these doctrines are a significant point of disagreement with our Jewish neighbors—it is one of the very real ways in which Jesus of Nazareth divides us, as he foretold. Second, I do not mean to imply that the promises of God have failed or will fail for the descendants of Israel, and I take no position here on the role of modern Israel and the Jewish people in the fulfillment of God's promises. Finally, I repudiate the hatred, persecution, and murder of Jews which have been done in the so-called name of Christ. The apostles warned against these things, and we must acknowledge with remorse that Christians have all too often failed to obey those warnings.

The New Testament makes it clear that the history of Israel from Abraham to Christ is no side-note. Jesus says of the law, the prophets, and the psalms that they speak of him (Luke 24:44), that his life and commandments express the entire law and prophets (Matt. 7:12), and that his coming does not abolish the law but fulfills it (Matt. 5:17). God's unchanging character, righteous and merciful, is manifest in the history of this chosen nation, and that history is the gateway to the gospel, as well as its foundation.

And the story of this chosen nation prior to the coming of Christ is crucial for understanding our lives today. It is not a model to be emulated or a blueprint for something like a Christian nation, but the opposite. It shows us clearly that *there can be no such thing as a Christian nation,* that the people of God are not defined nationally, culturally, or by any externally imposed marks or rules. That's because law—externally enforced—can't change hearts and belonging to God is a matter of the heart. We have seen this all-important truth in the prophets, in the teaching of Jesus, and in the apostolic foundations of the church. This is why Augustine's turn to religious legislation misrepresented the gospel, and indeed why all such attempts must do so.

It is ironic that Christians so often look to the model of Israel under the covenant of Moses to support religious legislation or to appeal for a nation belonging to God. Israel under the covenant of Moses is there to show us that law cannot change people's hearts, and therefore cannot produce a people for God. Remember Paul's rebuke to the churches of Galatia who sought to define the Christian community by law:

You foolish Galatians, who has bewitched you, before whose eyes Jesus Christ was publicly portrayed as crucified? This is the only thing I want to find out from you: did you receive the Spirit by the works of the Law, or by hearing with faith? Are you so foolish? Having begun by the Spirit, are you now being perfected by the flesh? (Galatians 3:1–3).

Have we been bewitched by the idea that there can be a Christian nation, tragically misusing a scriptural history designed to show us precisely the opposite? If so, the ones who suffer are our unbelieving neighbors, because we have hidden the gospel from them by misrepresentation.

Let me show this by considering another important objection to what I'm saying. "Christians *have* transformed hearts," some might rightfully insist. "The whole point of the new covenant in Jesus Christ is that the law is written on our hearts. Since this is true, couldn't there be a Christian nation if there were an earthly nation made up entirely of Christians?" We must of course acknowledge this possibility, but the sticking point seems fairly obvious: there aren't any nations like that. Augustine, you will remember, didn't even think there were any *churches* like that. All human institutions, he said, are mixed—they have believers and unbelievers (or maybe unbelievers only). Even if Augustine is wrong about churches, this certainly seems to be true of nations—human societies defined by geography, ethnicity, or law.

Suppose a group of Christians found a space and sought to set up a Christian nation. Sometimes we say that this is what a group of English Christians did in seventeenth century Massachusetts. But what happens when others come? Even if we leave aside the people already living in Massachusetts at that time (some of whom became Christians and some of whom did not), there are others. If a Christian nation has to have all Christians, what do we do with unbelievers? They could be killed (as some Quakers, who were considered unbelievers, were), or exiled (as Baptists, who were considered unbelievers, were). We could even do that with unbelieving children. But is that our mission to unbelievers? Aren't we suppose to preach the gospel to them?

Suppose, then, that we allowed unbelievers to stay in our Christian nation, provided that they follow the Christian laws we make. But, as I argued in the discussion of religious legislation, this seems incompatible with preaching the gospel because it obscures the gospel by presenting association with the people of God as an external matter, a matter of law. Using laws to make people who aren't Christians live as if they are Christians will not save those people; and even if unbelievers obey such laws, it will obscure their only true hope for salvation.

So, even if there *could* be a Christian nation provided everybody in it was a Christian, there doesn't seem to be a way to guarantee that everybody in the nation is a Christian without denying true Christianity and returning to law as the marker for God's people. But law cannot make people righteous in their hearts. (If not even the law of Moses—given by God—could do that, surely the laws of kings and legislators can't do it.) It is vain to preach the gospel to our neighbors and try at the same time to make a "Christian nation," because the gospel shows why there can't be any such nation. If we think otherwise, we are as tragically "bewitched" as the Galatians. Christ is the end of the law.

I am not denying that Christianity is political. "Jesus is Lord" means that the state is not sovereign, and frustrates the demand for allegiance which the nations of the world hold as necessary for their security—and maybe their existence. So the Christian profession is a political profession. But that doesn't make Jesus an earthly king, doesn't make any nation "Christian," and it doesn't make the followers of Jesus political rulers. What it does is limit the state's hold on the followers of Jesus. That's not going to make Christians pirates or anarchists (though we could be—and have been—called that), because we will submit to the state and serve its just ends. But we won't submit because the state has absolute authority over us—it doesn't. We'll do it in submission to God. Since our submission to God requires us first and foremost to worship God and proclaim the gospel, we are obligated to make sure that our political engagement does not falsely represent God (as an earthly king) or the gospel (as conditions that can be imposed by law).

We've discussed those pitfalls at some length up to this point; but how should we positively conceive our role in the kingdoms of the world so as to avoid them? That's our next question, and the answer is: as foreigners in the lands where we live.

Take this with you:

❖ Since external force (including the Law of Moses and the ordinances of Israel) cannot change the hearts of subjects, the history of Israel from Moses to Jesus is a story of repeated and inevitable apostasy because the people were "uncircumcised in heart."

❖ The promise of the new covenant was that the law of God would be written on the hearts of God's people, and the promise to Abraham was that this blessing would come to people of all nations. Jesus fulfills both promises.

❖ Old Testament Israel is not a model for a Christian nation—in fact, it is a warning against the possibility of a Christian nation. The people of God are not, and cannot be, nationally defined.

V.

Exiles on Main Street

You weren't a priest or a religious leader—just a shopkeeper, a farmer, a weaver. You lived under the law of Moses as best you could ... or as well as your neighbors. With your family you tried to be faithful, celebrating feasts when you could afford it, mostly making your tithes, not hurting anybody, trying to get along.

When the prophets came from God they spoke to the kings and the religious leaders, reminding them of the words of Moses who promised a curse if the people "do not listen to the commandments of the Lord your God, but turn aside from the way which I am commanding you." Righteous leaders saw the creeping corruption and cried to God to cleanse the land. "Oh I will," said God, and the words of the prophet Habakkuk spread among the people; even you heard the dreadful promise: "I am accomplishing a work in your days—you would not believe it even if you were told! I am raising up the Chaldeans, that grim and impetuous people who march throughout the earth, to take possession of dwelling places that are not theirs. They are terrifying and feared."

Nobody needed the prophet to add, "Be horrified! Be frightened speechless!" You all were. The Chaldeans! The bitterest enemies of small nations swallowed in their spreading empire. The armies of Babylon, with no knowledge or concern for the God of Israel, except to rob God's temple and to exact tribute from God's people. How could God give the people over to this evil empire? Yes, the northern kingdom of Israel had been swept away a century ago by the Assyrians, but you were part of the remnant — the kingdom of Judah, keepers of the temple, faithful to God and to Moses. God would not — could not — sweep you away by the Babylonians.

But even Habakkuk admitted it, his words like some nightmare song of dread:

I heard, and my inner parts trembled;
At the sound, my lips quivered.
Decay enters my bones,
And in my place I tremble;
Because I must wait quietly for the day of distress,
For the people to arise who will attack us.

And the day of distress did come. At first, you and your family didn't see much of it. Nebuchadnezzar himself led the attack on Judah, captured the king and took him away — putting the king's uncle Zedekiah on the throne. But Zedekiah thought it was safe to revolt against Babylon, and Nebuchadnezzar came back, killed Zedekiah's sons before his eyes, then blinded him and led him away in chains to Babylon. And soon the calamity came to you. The Babylonian captains came and burned the temple and the great houses of Jerusalem. They gathered the rest of the treasures of king and temple, and the people of the city, and took them to Babylon. A few poor farmers and vinedressers were left, and a few people in hiding, but not you. Your family was gathered and marched the long tearful journey — 600 miles across the eastern desert lands to the great rivers of Chaldea. Babylon.

How could the people of Israel be here? How could the temple of God lie in ruins and the city of Jerusalem in desolation? Had God abandoned Israel? And if these questions were too great for you, what were you supposed to do now? So far, you were getting by, your family beginning to scratch out a living among the exiles by the river Chebar, near the city.

And still the prophets spoke, and still the word filtered down even to families like yours. Ezekiel came with the imprisoned exiles, though Jeremiah escaped and remained in Judah. Another prophet in Judah, Hananiah, and some prophets among the exiles tried to give you and your neighbors hope. "Within two years," they said, "the Lord will break the yoke of Nebuchadnezzar! The Lord will restore the vessels of the temple and all the exiles to Judah. Within two years the king of Babylon will be thrown down!" What welcome news! What breath of relief! The word began to spread as it was gladly received. Yes, some worried that it didn't fully line up with other prophecies, but those were from long ago—in Judah before the invasion. Going home within two years! That's a message to pass along, and pass along it did.

Back in Judah, though, Jeremiah had a different message. Twenty years earlier, he was the one who had prophesied that Judah would be captive to Babylon for seventy years, and the Lord was confirming that word to him now. "Listen now, Hananiah," Jeremiah challenged. "The Lord has not sent you, and you have made this people trust in a lie. Therefore, this is what the Lord says: 'Behold, I am going to remove you from the face of the earth. This year you are going to die, because you have counseled rebellion against the Lord.'" Sure enough, Hananiah died in the seventh month of that year, but even before that, Jeremiah sent a letter to the people of God in Babylon to correct the false prophecy. That's the word that came, eventually, to you, to your family, to your neighbors:

This is what the Lord of armies, the God of Israel,
says to all the exiles whom I have sent into exile

from Jerusalem to Babylon: "Build houses and live
in them; and plant gardens and eat their produce.
Take wives and father sons and daughters, and take
wives for your sons and give your daughters to
husbands, so that they may give birth to sons and
daughters; and grow in numbers there and do not
decrease. Seek the welfare of the city where I have
sent you into exile, and pray to the Lord in its
behalf; for in its welfare will be your welfare." For
this is what the Lord of armies, the God of Israel
says: "Do not let your prophets who are in your
midst or your diviners deceive you, and do not
listen to their interpretations of your dreams which
you dream. For they prophesy falsely to you in
My name; I have not sent them," declares the Lord.
For this is what the Lord says: "When seventy
years have been completed for Babylon, I will visit
you and fulfill My good word to you, to bring you
back to this place."

*Yes, it was kind of a rude awakening, and truth be told not everybody
welcomed the message. Seventy years! You and your spouse wouldn't
live that long—maybe not even your children would. You will die in
exile, here in Babylon. The ones going back to Judah someday, to live as
God's people in the land of promise, will be born in Babylon most of them.
Still, the word of the Lord in the letter from Jeremiah seemed to fit better
with the prophecies from long ago—dark though they were. And, now
you know what to do. Settle down. Start your business back up; help the
exiles around you; and help the city you're in now—do your part for all
your neighbors, even those that aren't part of the people of God. Maybe
when you're settled, you or your kids will work alongside them, take part
in their civic affairs.*

But don't settle down too much. Don't forget that, although God put you in this land, this isn't God's land and it isn't your land. You're an exile here, even when your family becomes part of this society. Don't become so much a part that you forget your true citizenship, in Judah.

Because you have to teach the children born in Babylon that they are citizens of Judah too. *They won't have seen it—just heard stories from the old folks among the exiles. They'll have to know from you. They'll grow up in Babylon; they'll be a part of the city and work in the system, and maybe they'll marry and plant gardens here too. But they'll have to know that it isn't their city, and that God is going to take them, or their children, back to Judah. They'll be tempted to make Babylon their own, because it's hard to live as a stranger and an exile in the land where you are born. They might forget Judah, throw off the ways that the old teachers give them—the ways that make them different, the ways that remind them they are aliens. That's why you can't settle down too much; you can't forget your true citizenship; you have to keep the community of exiles—the citizens of Judah—alive and vibrant for the children born in Babylon. While you are working for the good of the city where God has placed you in exile, you must keep alive your hope for another city—your true citizenship—for your children and for the community of aliens. The testimony of God will endure in Babylon because the people of God in Babylon know it isn't their city.*

Seek the welfare of the city
where I have sent you into exile

(Jeremiah 29:7).

If we look to ancient Israel to find the mission of the modern church, the model is not the national glory of Israel, but the Babylonian captivity. In a kingdom where the least are greatest, the first are last, and the greatest are servants, maybe it isn't crazy to suppose that the Babylonian captivity tells us more about the church than all the more glorious aspirations of Israel as a nation. After all, Christians live in nations that cannot be Christian, and we need a biblical model for our relation to those nations and their laws. The Babylonian exile is that model, and the prophetic words to the exiles, what we know of their experience, and the relevance of their circumstances provide powerful and hopeful guidance for our own faithful life among the nations.

Taking the Babylonian captivity as a model isn't a narrow or idiosyncratic interpretive strategy. The people of God have been characterized as exiles and aliens in scripture from Abraham to the New Testament church. Centuries *before* Israel existed, Abraham "lived as an alien in the land of promise," and his descendants "died in faith, without receiving the promises, but having seen and welcomed them from a distance, and having confessed that they were strangers and exiles on the earth." (Hebrews 11:9,13). Centuries *after* the Babylonian exile, the apostle Peter addresses members of young churches as those "who reside as strangers," scattered throughout the provinces of Asia Minor. Even as Peter calls them "a chosen people for God's own possession," he urges them "as foreigners and strangers" to live exemplary lives submitted for the Lord's sake to the human institutions in which (and under which) they live (1 Peter 1-2).

Peter's advice to these early Christians is based on a clear principle: their identity is entirely fixed by their heavenly citizenship. They are who they are because of Jesus Christ, a "stone" rejected by the builders of the world, but made the "cornerstone" of a new kingdom by the one who made the world. And so they are in the world (and the regions of Pontus, Galatia, Cappadocia, Asia, and Bithynia) but they are not of it. They serve their neighbors, and contribute to society, family, culture, and "every human institution," but they do it as people whose allegiance lies elsewhere—with God who has made them "a chosen generation, a royal priesthood, a holy nation, a people for God's own possession," so that *they may proclaim the excellencies of him who has called them out of darkness into his marvelous light.*

Such was the beginning of the church, scattered in an empire which it did not make and could not call its own, because of the transformation wrought by Christ. This matches—in a profoundly deeper way—the circumstances of Israel in Babylon. Peter's instructions resonate fully with Jeremiah's words to Israel in exile: "Seek the welfare of the city where I have sent you into exile, and pray to the Lord on its behalf; for in its welfare you will have welfare." (Jer. 29:7). The prophet's message was two-fold: First, it was not God's intention to remove them from that nation while it lasted, and that they should seek the welfare of that nation as their home. But, second, God ultimately *would* remove them from that nation because it was not their actual home. On this model we have a basis upon which to work alongside our neighbors for the good of those neighbors and the land in which we live, but with the clear understanding that we are aliens in the land, with our true citizenship elsewhere.

So, this model gives us clear and unambiguous encouragement to take part in the affairs of our world, with a focus on the well-being of our neighbors. Recall the language from Augustine we used in chapter three to describe the role of Christians in temporal affairs: "common cause." Exiles have common cause with the citizens of the cities where they live, though they do not have common citizenship. The lives of exiles, then, are divided: we share the temporal concerns of our neighbors (everybody needs food, shelter, roads, water, political stability, etc.), but unlike our neighbors we have concerns that are unique to the kingdom of our true citizenship—the kingdom of God. This doesn't mean that our lives are divided; addressing the shared temporal concerns of our neighbors is simply fulfilling the command of our King to love our neighbors as ourselves. We do not have to share their allegiance to the earthly city in order to share their burden for temporal needs.

Jesus captured this fully when he said that we are in the world but not of the world. This model allows us to see this—and to see the dangers of forgetting that we are not of this world. We need not be ashamed of our temporal needs, and we can freely affirm that our shared humanity unites us with all who are subject—body and soul—to the brokenness of the world. But we are not of the world, and we must respond to its challenges in faithfulness to our King even when our neighbors—and our cities—do not. Consider those exiles of Israel who did not forget their true citizenship even while serving in the government of Babylon. Daniel and three fellow exiles in that service determined that they would not defile themselves with food that was, for the people of Judah, unclean. They managed to make an arrangement which satisfied their conscience and the king and continued to serve. Later circumstances (recorded in Daniel chapters 3 and 6) found the exiles unable to serve Babylon without violating their primary citizenship, and they refused to do that, even when threatened with death. They were *in* Babylon, but they were not *of* Babylon. May God give us the wisdom to discern what it looks like to be faithful to the kingdom of God in *our* cities of exile, and the strength to remain faithful, like those who have gone before us—not just in the face of death, but also of those lesser penalties that seem so big: loss of prestige, money, or institutional position. Those threats signal our status as exiles, aliens in the lands where we live. The ways of our kingdom are not the ways of the kingdoms in which we live. Forgetting this is perilous to our testimony and our calling.

But is it always easy to know where to join the city and where to keep ourselves apart? It's easy to know we shouldn't bow down to a giant golden statue of the king (though it may not be easy to follow through on that knowledge). But other issues may be more difficult to discern. What does it mean, in our times and the nations where we live, to be faithful to the kingdom of God in our lives, our work, and our testimony? We must, of course, seek to be filled with the Holy Spirit, and by the Spirit to understand the scriptures—given to us for that very purpose. When we differ from other Christians about where to draw the line, we must follow our conscience and we must not urge others to violate their conscience. This is the apostle Paul's exhortation on the matter, given in response to the controversial question of whether Christians in the Roman Empire should eat meat that had been sacrificed to idols.

Paul's teaching about faithful behavior for Christian exiles emphasizes individual conscience, scripture, and the Holy Spirit. But he has an additional focus which is crucial in the context of this question: the body of Christ. Christian exiles, just like the Babylonian exiles, don't face life merely as individuals scattered in a land whose ways are hostile to their true kingdom. There is a *community* of exiles, able to negotiate life as aliens *together* because of their shared citizenship in the kingdom of God. My own discernment can be confused, by my partial knowledge, by my own self-interest, by the limits of my perspective and experience. The shared life of Christian believers can and should clarify our discernment and deepen our understanding of the scriptures and our sensitivity to the Spirit. This is the function of the church; this is why the body of Christ—the community of believers—is essential to the Christian life. Understanding Christian life as aliens in exile from our true kingdom should vitalize and focus our understanding of the church.

It can be too easy in the modern world to think of "church" as something like a social organization or club of which we are a member. Of course local churches function in some regards like these other institutions which we and our neighbors, Christian or not, may be part of. But when we truly understand our circumstances, we see that the church (both the universal church and our local body) must be more than this. We are citizens of another kingdom, aliens in a land whose ways are fundamentally different from ours because of the fallenness of the world and of all nations. The church is the community of exiles, and in it we must learn the ways of our true land, we must pass them on, and *we must represent them to the land where we live in exile.*

This vision of the church as a community of exiles is powerfully expressed by Stanley Hauerwas and Will Willimon, who write that the church is not "a service club within a generally Christian culture, but … a *colony* within an *alien society*." In *Resident Aliens: Life in the Christian Colony*, Hauerwas and Willimon affirm the true power and essential character of the church in the world:

> Christian community, life in the colony, is not primarily about togetherness. It is about the way of Jesus Christ with those whom he calls to himself. It is about disciplining our wants and needs in congruence with a true story, which gives us the resources to lead truthful lives. In living out the story together, togetherness happens, but only as a by-product of the main project of trying to be faithful to Jesus.[7]

This community and the fact that it is alien to the societies in which we live does not cut us off from those societies. We are called to love our neighbors, to lay down our lives, to proclaim the kingdom of God, and to show that kingdom in our transformed lives. Identifying ourselves, as modern Christians, with the command to "seek the good of the city where I have placed you in exile" should energize our mission and vitalize our churches.

And we need this energy and vitality, because life as exiles is not easy for those who insist on affirming their true citizenship in a kingdom which is so different from their exile home. It is hard to not fit in. If we cling to the ways of our true kingdom, we are tempted either to take over, or to retreat. Understanding ourselves as a community of exiles helps us to avoid those errors, as well as the temptation to give up—to conform ourselves to the ways of the cities in which we live as aliens. And if this is hard for *us*, how difficult it must be for our children!

---

7 Stanley Hauerwas and William H. Willimon, *Resident Aliens: Life in the Christian Colony* (Expanded 25th Anniversary Edition) (Nashville: Abingdon Press, 2014) pp. 115, 78.

Think of those parents in Babylon. Their children are born there, and perhaps will die there. Yet they must understand their true citizenship, because God has promised that the captives will return to Judah and restore the temple and the land. Until then, those children must fulfill the command of God to work for the good of the city where they live in exile—*without giving up and simply becoming Babylonians like their neighbors*. May God renew the inspiration for our churches to be, by the Holy Spirit, genuine communities of transformed lives, where we and our children know a new way, a different way, and serve the world as Christ served the world.

Jesus, we may be reminded, said that he *overcame* the world. Too often the church has attempted to overcome the world by the world's own means—to literally take over the nations in which the church resides as an alien community. But nations—unlike the kingdom of our God—are ruled by swords. Though he will bear a rod and sword at the end of the age, Jesus did not overcome the world by its own means. He lifted no sword to overcome the world. In his kingdom, authority means the opposite of the world's use of authority. Followers of a crucified Lord will not, and should not, fit in this world—but, like Jesus, they can embrace it, and serve it. Freeing ourselves from attempting to *possess* the lands in which we live, embracing our identity as exiles in those lands, opens to us, collectively and individually, the possibility of being to them as Jesus was. And as we do this in Christ's way—not the way of the nations and their chiefs—we literally reveal the power and the grace of the kingdom of our God. We live lives which testify of our King; we fulfill our high calling.

But what does this look like in practice, especially as we engage with the institutions, the governments, and the economies of the nations in which we live? As we conclude this meditation, let's turn to a few ideas about that.

Take this with you:

❖ The Babylonian exile of Israel is the best biblical model for understanding the relation of Christians to the nations in which we live.

❖ Working for the good of our neighbors, and participating in the institutions of the societies where we live reflects the prophetic call to seek the good of the city where God has placed us in exile while remaining faithful to our true citizenship in another kingdom.

❖ The church is not simply another social organization, but a community of exiles, living in shared purpose to remember our true citizenship, and to make that other kingdom known.

Christian Witness
and Political Action

*For you have been called for this purpose, because Christ
also suffered for you, leaving you an example, so that you
would follow in His steps, He who committed no sin,
nor was any deceit found in His mouth; and while being
reviled, He did not revile in return; while suffering, He
uttered no threats, but kept entrusting Himself to the One
who judges righteously*

(1 Peter 2:21–23).

What do they look like, these exiles in Babylon? How do they
seem to their neighbors, their co-workers, their political allies and
opponents in this land where they live as aliens? Some accuse
them of hating the city, but they don't, really—after all their good
is tied up with the good of the city ... at least, for the time that
they are in exile there. They do care about their neighbors and
the welfare of Babylon, and are willing to contribute to its political
life (though there are some things the exiles won't do—they are
different that way). When they do try to help out with the affairs

of the city, just like all the regular citizens they don't always agree with each other about the best plans or policies. But there's something different about that too—their political disagreements with each other don't disrupt their unity and their solidarity as an exile community. They don't let the politics of Babylon take precedence over their life as the people of Israel—though they are stuck in that foreign land. Their unity, that community, has a depth and permanence that people notice. Some say they love each other, and that's how you can tell they're loyal to a foreign King.

And in spite of how different that exile community is, they invite their Babylonian neighbors to join it. Mind you, they don't try to turn Babylon into their land—that's impossible. But they welcome their neighbors to change allegiance and join the exiles. This is, at least, slightly subversive and, as you can imagine, the Babylonian powers-that-be don't like it. That doesn't surprise the aliens. They know this isn't their land, and they understand that they (their King really) threaten it. If the Babylonians can get the exiles to think of the city as their own—get them invested in running the place—they'll be easier to control, less of a threat … just one more Babylonian political party. But the exiles resist, heroically though it doesn't usually look that way, sticking to what they know, emulating the humility of their King, doing the right thing, and encouraging each other as the day of their liberation draws near.

The vision of Christians as exiles in the nations where we live is at the heart of all that I have attempted to say about our participation in politics and government. I don't pretend to have answered—or even tried to answer—all the hard questions that a biblical theology of politics must address. And I certainly haven't tried to say what laws Christians should pass, what economic policies Christians should support, what side Christians should take in specific political policy disputes—beyond such generalities as saying that we should not use laws to try to get people who aren't Christians to act as if they are, and that there may not always be a single policy that all Christians should support. Vision is broader than all that but no less important; without vision, the Proverbs say, we lack guidance, we're unrestrained, we perish. When Jesus said to Pilate, *"If my kingdom were of this world, then my servants would be fighting,"* he was saying to all of us, his followers, that the way we face the kingdoms of the world is evidence for the kind of kingdom we serve. Our actions, including our political actions, must be guided by a vision of the kingdom of God, its relation to the nations, and our place in it.

So, having attempted to evoke a vision, let me conclude by talking briefly about our actions. Questions about how Christians act in the world are as important to our witness as what political decisions we make. What does it mean to act like a Christian in family, school, church, and—most importantly for this meditation—politics?

Here's a simple example: Christians don't lie or use double standards. That's straightforward enough. False witness, according to scripture, is an abomination to God—so are "differing weights and differing measures." But is this so easy? Let's look a little closer. Aren't we sometimes tempted to obscure the truth *for the sake of our witness?* Too often ministries or their leaders get into trouble and realize (correctly) that this is bad for the reputation of that ministry and maybe even the reputation of Christianity and the gospel. That realization then motivates us to hide the facts, to dodge the questions, to stretch the truth, and sometimes even to lie outright. We could of course avoid all this by not getting into trouble (or even "the appearance of evil"), but I'm not throwing that stone here. Christianity is fundamentally about what happens when we fall.

Look, the kingdoms and the institutions of the world don't have any trouble with truth when all is well; but when things are down they have no recourse but to preserve their reputation, their appearance, their earthly gain—*because that is all they have.* One powerful enticement to deception in Christian ministries, and in Christians' individual lives, is when we come to think of our ministries, our lives, or our political ambitions in the same way that the world thinks of people and institutions. It is that deeper denial of the gospel which opens the door for us to deny the overt demand of scripture that we avoid false witness.

Of course we don't need mistaken institutional assumptions to lead us to sin. Our selfish nature does that quite well on its own. Let's think about double standards in that light, and look for ways to fight back. People have a natural tendency to believe comfortable falsehoods about the faults of others, and to *not* believe uncomfortable truths about their own failings. So we often paint our own motives in the best possible light, but are quick to disparage the motives of others. This leads directly to the application of double standards—especially when we disagree with others or stand to benefit by applying the standards that way. All people are subject to making this mistake, and it's really hard to see it when you are doing it; perspectives and judgments are distorted by desires. Knowing this, Christians—since we abhor false measures even though tempted to use them—should *choose* to question comfortable claims about others, especially those who aren't like us (or those who don't like us). And we should *choose* to listen non-defensively when uncomfortable claims are made about us. This commitment won't solve the problems of broken persons making judgments in broken institutions, but it's an effort to make things better; more importantly, it is essential to our witness.

What about non-defensiveness in general? Shouldn't that be central to our witness? I don't mean refusing to stand up for anything, I mean not being afraid to admit our imperfection—including the possibility that we are mistaken or have done wrong. Christians should be first in line not just to say this, but to act as if we really believe it. After all, our very identity as Christians begins with the realization that we have failed, through our own fault, to satisfy the righteousness of God. We acknowledge the justice of God's judgment against us, and marvel at the fact that in spite of all that, God not only loves us but welcomes us to fellowship—via a path made possible at great cost *to God*. We have not earned this astonishing gift, and even when yet again we fail morally, it remains open if we repent. "If we confess our sins, God is faithful and righteous to forgive us our sins and to cleanse us from all unrighteousness." That is the foundation of our life in Christ.

In spite of all this, we are still afraid to be wrong. When problems arise in our relationships, it is hard to entertain the thought—even harder to *say*—"this might be my fault." It is much easier to be defensive, to fight back. When those of us who are white hear from our black neighbors that a society controlled by white people has disadvantaged them, we get defensive—even though we didn't create that society. When we learn that our group, our country, even our historic church did not do the right thing, we get defensive; we go on the attack. I'm not saying that "our group" is always wrong or that our accusers are always right; that's not true and we should love the truth. But defensiveness—fear of being wrong—can keep us from seeing what *is* true; I am talking about our attitudes and our approach to things. Christians should boldly testify that we are aware of our imperfection, and that we know our value does not come from always being right. And we testify MOST LOUDLY to that when we act like we believe it. Since we are free (unimaginably free from the perspective of our neighbors) to admit we might be wrong, let's stop before we answer an accusation with an accusation in a relationship. We can just pause and ask ourselves, "Could I be wrong here?" before we speak. In the great social debates of our time, where blame is placed on racial groups, economic ideologies, religious movements that we might be part of, let's stop and *listen* to those who say we are part of the problem. If they are right, we need to listen; and if they are wrong, *we can afford to listen*, and to do it with genuine openness. This is not agreeing in advance with criticism, it is using our tremendous Christian freedom to listen in humility and openness. People will notice—especially, in these times in which we live. And what they notice will tell them something about the gospel of Jesus Christ.

Would this make things look different? What if Christians in politics never lied or slanted the story to make themselves look good or others look bad? What if we were careful to apply the same standards to ourselves or our group as we do to others and—to help make sure we were—we listened non-defensively to our opponents' views about whether we were doing it? What if we were quicker to acknowledge that we might be wrong, and slower to attribute evil motives to others—even when we publicly disagree with them? What if we did not act as if success or failure in business, politics, or finance were matters of ultimate importance? *What if we showed that we believe it is better to do the right thing and lose than to do the wrong thing and win?*

One thing about these proposals (which many Christians habitually practice): they aren't exactly a recipe for success in the institutions that surround us. Recently I heard someone comment, "In a nation where decency is dead, if you try to be nice, you will be used as a doormat." This is an insightful and important observation. It gets to the heart of the essential thing for Jesus followers to understand about politics in this world. When Jesus said, "My kingdom is not of this world," he didn't mean that the kingdom of God wasn't real, and he didn't mean that his followers should withdraw from the world. He meant the kingdom of God is *radically different.* He sends his followers into the world and says, "I send you out as lambs in the midst of wolves." Jesus does not mean lambs with hidden wolf-teeth to beat them at their own game. He means lambs like he was a lamb among wolves. The wolves killed him.

> He was oppressed and He was afflicted,
> Yet He did not open His mouth;
> Like a lamb that is led to slaughter,
> And like a sheep that is silent before its shearers,
> So He did not open His mouth. (Isaiah 53:7)

I am not claiming for a second that *we* are the precious Lamb of God slain for the sins of the world. But we are his witnesses, and we are his followers, and he sends us out as lambs in the midst of wolves ... and if we die, then we die. Perhaps even harder: if we look like fools, then we look like fools; if we lose an argument because we will not cheat or lose an election because we will not lie, then we lose those things.

The great temptation of the church (through time and in our time) has been to think that we must resist the world on the world's terms. But doing that, we deny—with our very lives—that there is another kingdom which we serve. Our lives must testify to a crucified Lord. The power of the cross is hidden to the wisdom of the world; we proclaim that power by following our Lord, though the way of Jesus looks as foolish to our societies as it did to Pilate.

The most important thing about Christian political action is not who we vote for or what policy positions we take, but whether in our action we testify to the true Lord, the true King—whose kingdom is not of this world. Of course we genuinely seek the good of our neighbor, and policy makes a difference for that. But we must pursue those political goals as aliens in our land and citizens of another city—even if those alien ways seem doomed to fail in the nations where we are scattered. The end justifies the means only for those who have no hope. Will we abandon our witness to such hope for political achievement?

This is not business as usual. Nothing in the world today tells us to accept humiliation, to place the interests of others above our own, to accept defeat rather than to bear false witness. Maybe I should say, nothing *of* the world tells us this. But Jesus not only shows the way, he tells his followers how to live in this world as citizens of another kingdom. This means orienting ourselves to the reality of God's kingdom—whatever that looks like in this world.

Such an orientation involves actual dependence upon God. We can see a simple illustration of this in the familiar verses of Matthew where Jesus warns against advertising one's charitable giving. "When you give to the poor," he says, "do not sound a trumpet before you, as the hypocrites do in the synagogues and in the streets, so that they may be honored by men. Truly I say to you, they have their reward in full. But when you give to the poor, do not let your left hand know what your right hand is doing, so that your giving will be in secret; and your Father who sees what is done in secret will reward you" (Matt. 6:2–4). Notice that allowing the good work to be known brings a reward—recognition, perhaps admiration. I've gotten this kind of reward, you probably have too, and of course I like it. Jesus doesn't even say it's bad—just that the reward you get is the end of it. But he also says that we can forgo the earthly payoff, keep our action secret, and God will reward the action.

The crucial point here is that following Jesus means depending, literally depending, on God for the reward—rather than on the payoff system all around us. "Literally depending" on God means: if God doesn't exist, there won't be a reward; without God, the secret gift trades the earthly reward for ... nothing. Here's another example: in the gospel of Mark, Jesus points out rich people giving lots of money to the temple, alongside a poor widow who gives a tiny offering. Jesus said that the poor widow put in more than all the contributors to the treasury. Why? "Because they all put in out of their surplus, but she, out of her poverty, put in all she owned, all she had to live on" (Mk. 12:44). Her action repudiated dependence on an economic system necessary—apart from God— for life. Although these examples are about money, the point isn't about the money—it's about depending on the reality of God and God's kingdom. This isn't trivial because if we do it, and God isn't real or God isn't what we thought, we lose.

Isn't this exactly what Jesus did in submitting to execution? He did not turn the weapons of the empire against the system that killed him, though he might have raised not just earthly armies but, according to his testimony, heavenly ones. He submitted himself to death, "by the hands of godless men," as Peter proclaimed on the day of Pentecost. But, "He was neither abandoned to Hades, nor did his flesh suffer decay. This Jesus God raised up again" (Acts 2:31–32). The great profession of the gospel is that this submission, and this great victory, is entirely at odds with the system of the world and represents a repudiation of the world's power and the world's ways.

And yet the power of God is so often unseen. Good people do the right thing and suffer. The wicked prosper, and God seems silent. The scriptures profess that God desires our good in this broken world, but we find pain, heartbreak, the death of loved ones who should outlive us. But wait! Of course the power of God is often unseen—it isn't a version of the world's power and it isn't on display as if it is.

> God has chosen the foolish things of the world to shame the wise, and God has chosen the weak things of the world to shame the things which are strong, and the base things of the world and the despised God has chosen, the things that are not, so that He may nullify the things that are (1 Corinthians 1:27–28).

What does this mean for success "in this world"? What does this mean for Christians in politics? It does not mean that the power of God is not real. We must in fact *depend* on the reality of God and God's power. We experience this at the very beginning of our call to follow Jesus. "It is due to Him that you are in Christ Jesus." This same passage continues, "Who became to us wisdom from God, and righteousness and sanctification, and redemption." And we live out this calling in the political and social cultures where God has placed us:

By devotion to the Savior, filled with the Spirit and growing in honesty, humility, compassion, and love for neighbor.

By the mutual encouragement of the body of Christ, the Church, which is a community of exiles bound together by our connection to God and one another through Jesus Christ, neither beholden nor conforming to the world around us.

By proclamation of the true hope of the world in the gospel of Jesus Christ, freely offered to our neighbors and culture without imposing it upon them—just as God presented it to us.

By participating in society and government as we are needed and allowed, careful to keep conscience clear in our primary devotion to God, and motivated to do good to our neighbors and protect everyone from injustice, as far as these systems are able to secure these ends.

Of course we are beset by temptation in the life of discipleship. Nearly all temptation is a form of self-interest: to be on the winning side; to be comfortable; to avoid responsibility for harm done; to gain power, privilege, wealth, recognition; to treat others as we do not want to be treated; to return evil for evil. Let's be open, each one of us, about our own struggles with these forms of self-love. Let's preserve an exile community that cares more about gently helping each other grow out of them than about having the right political affiliation or backing the right political policies.

Because in the end, the gospel of Jesus Christ depends upon God's transforming power in the lives of people in every nation—

not what nation we are in or what laws the nations adopt. Our political participation must testify to this above all else.

Take this with you:

❖ Actions like refusing to lie, use double standards, or react defensively—things which often seem necessary for political success—show that Christians serve a different kingdom and what that kingdom is like.

❖ Living according to the kingdom of God while in this world involves a dependence upon God which seems foolish to the world (and it is foolish if God and God's kingdom are not real).

❖ Whatever political actions we take, we must show what the kingdom of God is like by being in the world like Jesus was in the world, depending upon God and loving our neighbors.

A lamb,
standing as if slain.

When John the Revelator was caught up into heaven, he beheld
a scene of glory and the transcendent power of God. In the right
hand of the One who sat on the throne at the center of it all was
a book—but it was sealed and no one was found worthy to open it.

You will remember John's account, in the fifth chapter of the book
of Revelation, of his distress at this vision. But one of the heavenly
powers told him to stop weeping: *Behold, the Lion that is from the
tribe of Judah, the Root of David, has overcome so as to be able to open
the book.*

This moment—at the climax of the great sweep of human history,
divine retribution, and final reconciliation—is the most important
revelation of Jesus Christ for the purpose of our meditation on the
gospel and the nations of the world. John says:

> *And I saw between the throne and the elders a Lamb
> standing, as if slain.*

What kind of picture is this? In this setting of power—terrible and
awesome and mighty, burning earthly power into insignificance—

John turns to see the King of kings, the One who has overcome all earthly kingdoms and dominion. And what does he see? A lamb. A slain lamb. The most powerful ruler of earth is its gentlest creature--killed, but somehow standing. Nothing could more clearly show us that when Jesus said, "My kingdom is not of this world," he did not deny that he ruled the world. Rather, he declared that his authority was manifested in a way utterly foreign to the nations. What the nations call defeat was his victory, and not only did he overcome the kings of the earth in his death, but he purchased for God—with his blood—citizens *from every tribe and tongue and people and nation*, citizens of the kingdom of God.

What manner of people, then, should we be, here in exile among the nations? In the last hours before his execution, Jesus told his closest followers, *I have spoken to you so that in me you may have peace. In the world you have tribulation, but take courage; I have overcome the world.* They did not yet understand his resurrection to come; they would not know at first that his death was victory, not defeat. Sometimes it seems that we barely understand that now. But listen to his words: "I have overcome the world"—not *will* overcome—but *I have overcome the world.*

Jesus did not use armies—earthly or heavenly—to overcome the world. He did not use rulers, or laws, or the swords that back them up. Consider his ministry, recorded in the gospels: he *never raised his hand* against the world (against the moneychangers in the temple, yes, but that was "zeal for the house of God," not fighting the world on its terms). He did not agree with the world; he didn't accept or justify its corrupt behavior; he didn't turn a blind eye to its rebellion against God. He lived and spoke in a way that testified against the world. He commanded those who heard him to stop, to turn, to repent. We can say that Jesus raised his voice, but he did not raise his hand. And yet, he overcame the world.

Governments are ordained by God in this broken world to protect the innocent, to keep evil in check. But they cannot overcome evil. Jesus did, laying down his own life in dependence upon God. This is not the way of the world; it is the way of another world, another kingdom. "If my kingdom were of this world," Jesus said to the rulers who thought their power was the decisive element, "My servants would be fighting. But as it is, my kingdom is not of this realm." Let us, his servants today, remember that the kingdom of God did not open to us by the sword, but by a king standing as a slain lamb. And let our politics, if politics we must have, be stamped through and through with the mark of a *crucified* Lord, lest we hide the gospel of Jesus Christ for the sake of earthly power.